by

Ruth C. Forde
Nina L. Hayden
Mary J. Ottmann-Bass

COPYRIGHT

© Ruth C. Forde
Nina L. Hayden
Mary J. Ottmann-Bass
& Godzwow Publications, Inc. 2020

Authors: Ruth C. Forde, Nina L. Hayden
and Mary J. Ottmann-Bass

ruthceforde@gmail.com
ninalynnhayden@hotmail.com
bbass@tampabay.rr.com

Published by Godzwow Publications, Inc. 2020
www.godzwowpublications.com

In partnership with Godzwow, Inc.
www.godzwow.com

All Rights Reserved Internationally

Cover concept and design by Shaun Johnson,
SPJ Graphic Designs Inc.

Published in the United States
for worldwide distribution.
ISBN: 978-1-7348388-2-4

This book may not be copied or reprinted for commercial gain or profit. No part of this book may be reproduced or transmitted in any form or by any means, electronic or mechanical. No photocopying, recording, or storage and retrieval of any information may be done without permission in writing from the publisher. Please direct any and all inquiries to info@godzwowpublications.com

Unless indicated, Scripture references are taken from the King James Version of the Holy Bible.

CONTENTS

A COMPILATION OF MYSTIC PRAYERS	
COPYRIGHT	
DEDICATION	1
ACKNOWLEDGEMENTS	2
INTRODUCTION	3
SPEAKING LIFE	4
MOUTH GATE	5
THE AGE OF MELCHIZEDEK	6
THE SPIRIT OF THE FEAR OF THE LORD	7
ENGAGING THE BEING OF FAITH	8
EYE GATE	9
EXPANDING YOUR SPIRIT MAN	10
WORSHIP GATE	12
ACTIVATING YOUR IMAGINATION	13
REVERANCE GATE	14
LION	15
ANI (I AM)	16
EAR GATE	17
MOBILE COURT ENGAGEMENT	18
INTUITION GATE	20
HEART INTERCESSION	21

BUILDING THE HOPE GATE	22
CONSCIENCE GATE	23
COMMUNION PRAYER	24
OX	26
THE SPIRIT OF THE LORD	27
REASON GATE	28
UNTETHERING FROM TIME	30
ENGAGING THE ANGELIC REALM	32
STEPPING ON YOUR MOUNTAIN	33
WILL GATE	35
THE SPIRIT OF COUNSEL	36
NOSE GATE	37
EAGLE	39
ENGAGING THE THRONE OF GRACE	41
MY IMAGINATION AS A GATE	42
THE SPIRIT OF KNOWLEDGE	43
CHOICE GATE	44
MAN	45
OPENING MY LOVE GATE	46
ENGAGING THE GATE OF REVELATION	48
I AM A THREE-PART BEING	49
EMOTION GATE	51
ACTIVATING MY GODHOOD	52
THE SPIRIT OF WISDOM	53

I AM FREQUENCY	54
MIND GATE	55
REIGNING IN REST	56
WISDOM OF THE REALMS	57
HAND GATE	59
THE SPIRIT OF MIGHT	61
HEAVENLY TRADING	63
FEAR OF YHVH GATE	65
REFERENCES	67
ABOUT THE AUTHORS	75

DEDICATION

To Hashilush ha Kodesh.
WE LOVE YOU with
ALL of OUR Being.

ACKNOWLEDGEMENTS

"Uncle Ian Clayton," words cannot express our deepest love and gratitude for your stewarding the heart of Yahweh and sharing your profound encounters and engagements in His Kingdom Realms. We are eternally grateful.

"Big Brother," Marios Ellinas, your wisdom, knowledge, and engagements with the Kingdom Realms have had such an impact on our lives. Your encouragement has been priceless. We thank you and love you.

Corina Toncz-Pataki and Wendy Cooper, our "Blue Blood Sisters." What an honor and privilege it has been learning from you and co-laboring with you to bring the government of Yahweh on Earth as it is in Heaven. Together, Forever, Your Sisters.

INTRODUCTION

All of creation reveals the glory of Yahweh and His majesty, glory, and greatness!

This book is a compilation of prayers engaging with Heavenly Beings in the Kingdom Realms.

We are honored you would take the time to step into our journey as we open our hearts to share some of the most intimate prayers we have spoken.

We believe these prayers will be inspirational to you and have chosen to reveal them to the world for such a time as this.

As you read through these mystical prayers, engage with the Heavenly Beings, and use these prayers as a spiritual technology to develop your own prayers.

We, as Sons in Yahweh, have great joy in the blueprint He has created for humanity.

May your engagement with this book take you to places you have never seen before!

SPEAKING LIFE

Yahweh, I thank You for crowning me with glory and honor, and establishing me as a ruler over everything You have made, putting Your creation under my feet. (1) With that authority and power, I speak life, not death into my environment. (2) I have a pure heart because it is totally immersed into Yours, which reflects blessings that come out of my mouth. (3)

As Your Kingdom lives in me, whatever declarations I speak are fixed in my life. (4) My words, which are seeds, will be planted for Your Kingdom and produce an abundant harvest. (5) I will always speak what I mean. (6)

I am a Son of Yahweh, blessed everywhere my spirit expands itself. My family, home, work, and sphere of influence carries the vibration, frequency, and sound of the heart of Yahweh. Your government rests upon my shoulders because I am like You. (7)

MOUTH GATE

Yahweh, in obedience to You, I speak, and things manifest in my life. From my seat on my mountain, I measure my words, and they nourish those who are listening. (1) Each word coming out of my mouth is a gift, building up and encouraging others because I do not engage in unsavory talk. (2) I am always careful of what I say, so blessings and not calamity are my reward. (3)

My goal in every conversation allows the best in others to be seen. (4) I never say anything evil nor hurtful because my desire is to draw others to the glory that is YHVH.

As I speak, my heart is listening and obeying.

As I speak, chaos disappears.

As I speak, Yahweh is magnified.

As I speak, Yahweh's Kingdom manifests on the Earth. (5)

THE AGE OF MELCHIZEDEK

This moment I choose to step into the Age of Melchizedek.

I leave behind religion, its old framework, platforms, and mindsets of those whom I have chosen to learn from.

This moment I choose to be a Priest under the order of Melchizedek.

I choose the pathway of Sonship to be tutored by the 7 Spirits of Yahweh and my Governors, and I willingly give my trades and leveraging to the treasures of The Kingdom.

I am willing to learn and engage in what it means to be an Oracle, King, and Legislator.

I understand Yahweh has a blueprint and a living scroll for me, and I willingly choose to surrender to its dictates in my life.

Yahweh, use me as an instrument for Your Glory. Yeshua, I embody Your sacrifice and grace. Ruach ha Kodesh, Your power is present and moving in me. (1)

THE SPIRIT OF THE FEAR OF THE LORD

I turn the intent of my heart to befriend and call upon you Spirit of the Fear of the Lord whose color is purple.

You are the fountain of life who turns me away from evil. (1)

Knowing you, I am known to Yahweh, Who rewards me with riches honor and life. (2)

Teach me holiness, righteousness, and intimacy in Yahweh.

My life is perfected through you, bringing me wisdom, knowledge, and understanding.

In you is a place of refuge where I can rest satisfied untouched by harm. (3)

You are my treasure. (4)

ENGAGING THE BEING OF FAITH

According to the words of Yeshua, Ruach ha Kodesh and Yahweh, whatever I speak, will become a reality on Earth and throughout the Cosmos.

I engage with you, Being of Faith, to learn from you and embody you in my thoughts, actions, and deeds. My Faith moves any obstacles, takes me through any circumstance, because I have full and complete trust in Yahweh. Nothing is impossible for me. (1)

Yahweh, you never lie nor change your mind. (2) As I stand righteous before Your throne (3), I take the keys of the Kingdom that have been given to me and open Your storehouse. (4) As I embody Faith, I meditate on Yeshua and experience prosperity and success. (5)

At this moment, I live an ever-increasing, vibrant Faith.

EYE GATE

Yahweh, I thank You that I am spiritually perceptive.

My eyes are lamps, and my body is full of light. (1) This light prevents me from stumbling, so I always make good choices.

My eyes lead me on the path to Sonship.

Because I made an agreement with my eyes (2), I never look at anything that is wicked or worthless. (3) My eyes are always open to see the needs of others so that I can assist and bless them.

My desire is to see the angelic host of Heaven, so I speak to my eyes, be open, and see the angels all around me. I use windows to look through, and because my eyes are the windows to my soul, I focus on things that are positive and uplifting, which matures my soul.

My eyes are always clear, and my vision is powerful. As I open my eyes, I see the realm of the Kingdom to read my destiny scroll.

Yahweh, I praise and thank You for clear vision. (4)

EXPANDING YOUR SPIRIT MAN

I engage with my sanctified imagination to see my spirit being.

I expand my spirit to the outside of my body and surround every facet of my body giving it an embrace.

As my spirit holds my body, I turn the intent of my heart to Yahweh and allow the love of Yahweh to flow from His heart through my spirit being to my body.

I wait for refreshing.

I wait for healing.

I expand my spirit man to the outside of my home. I use my sanctification imagination to pull my home into my belly.

Out of my belly flows rivers of living water into my home. (1)

I brood over my home.

I bring my home into alignment with Yahweh's

heart.

My body and home are filled with the love of Yahweh. (2)

WORSHIP GATE

Yahweh, I come into Your presence and bow low before Your throne. I offer you all of me. You are glorious, full of truth and holiness.

Your goodness abounds throughout Realms upon Realms, upon Realms.

I adore You; I honor You; I worship You.

I enter in with the Angelic Hosts and Heavenly Beings. We sing Your praises in the midst of the thundering crescendos of HOLY, HOLY, HOLY.

Yeshua, You are unspeakably beautiful. You are majestic and reign as the King of Kings. Yeshua, Yeshua, I LOVE YOU.

I inhale and exhale your essence, Ruach ha Kodesh. I embody Your translucent purity. Your joy is my strength and my covering. I worship You from the beginning forever and ever. (1)

ACTIVATING YOUR IMAGINATION

Thank You, Yahweh, for the gift of my imagination, which reflects Your creativity and glory.

I frame my imagination and bring it before You. I wash it with the blood of Yeshua and paint it until it is clean and turns into white light.

I step through the frame of my imagination with one of the Godhead (Hashilush Ha Kodesh) to engage with the Heavenly Realms.

I can see with the eyes of my heart from the inside out. I can see my heart beating as one with Yours, and I feel the frequency of Your love vibrating over, around, and through me.

I covenant to use my imagination for Your will, purposes, and glory.

REVERANCE GATE

I step through the gate of reverence to honor You, Hashilush ha Kodesh.

I open my heart in devotion and submit myself to You.

I am awestruck by Your name. (1)

I fall on my face before You, and I am made flawless in Your love. (2)

For as I live, I live for You, Lord. I belong to You. (3)

I will Trust in You Yahweh, Forever, for You are my rock. (4)(5)

LION

I engage with the face of the Lion. (1)

The roar of the Lion vibrates through the framework of my being penetrating every atom and cell.

It resonates with the calling to step into something greater.

I am called to be a King.

I am called to rule, protect, and establish the boundaries of the Kingdom of YHVH on Earth as it is in Heaven.

Inside me resonates the authority, dominion, and fear of the presence of YHVH.

I operate alongside the Spirit of the Lord and the Spirit of the Fear of The Lord.

Together we accomplish the purposes of Hashilush ha Kodesh on the Earth and throughout the Cosmos.

I am the Lion.

Hear me ROAR.

ANI (I AM)

I am that I am who Yahweh created me to be.

My body is perfect, without spot or blemish, and I see myself how Yeshua sees me. (1)

Body, I respect and honor you for the being you were created to be.

I ask for forgiveness if I have spoken or treated you in a way that is dishonoring.

You are a temple created in the image of Yahweh. (2)

I love you and covenant to nourish and protect you.

Ruach ha Kodesh, thank you for living in my body, restoring it to its original creation.

Body, you are a being of light.

The frequency, sound, and fragrance of my cells vibrate in-tune with Yahweh as we are One.

Forever.

Together.

EAR GATE

Yahweh, I thank You for opening my ears to Your instruction and discipline (1) to mature me on this Sonship journey. My ear is always attuned to wisdom, which leads me to understanding.

My priories are insightful and positive. (2)

I am always listening for the voice of Ruach ha Kodesh; whenever I get off track, I hear "this is the right road, walk down it." (3) I pay attention to what I hear because it is helping me to study and become wise as I respond to what I am learning. (4)

Today I choose to step into Your heart Yahweh, and I hear You speak to me in gentle whispers. As I listen, You give instructions for accomplishing what is written on my scroll and how to walk it out.

I know the voice of Yeshua, my Elder Brother Who, helps and instructs me as a Lord, then a Priest, and a King ruling from my mountain.

I have an ear, and I will always listen to and obey the voice of Hashilush ha Kodesh. (5)

MOBILE COURT ENGAGEMENT

Yahweh, I come to You into the Mobile Court of Heaven, and I admit and repent of...

(Name the specific sin in the generational line in your DNA and/or BLOODLINE that has been ruling in your life, and apply it ALL the way back to the record when it was first created through trading by your generational line with evil beings or overshadowing by evil beings into your generational line.)

I thank You, Yahweh that I am covered by the blood of Yeshua, and UNDER this covering, I ask that You Judge me for the sins my ancestors and I have committed.

Now that I have been judged, I ask the bailiff angels to bring in every evil being that participated in these sins, and I ask that You judge them...

(Tell Yahweh what you want done to them - burnt to a crisp, sent to the abyss, sent to the pit forever etc..)

Thank you, Yahweh, I turn away, and divorce myself from these sins and I ask for a divorce decree that

You and I will sign.

I turn my eyes to You and covenant to.... (now tell Yahweh what you will do instead of the sin, for example instead of fear I will have Faith, etc.)

Yahweh, I now ask for an edict that I may use to enforce this judgment today to administrate it in my life according to Your Will.

(Now speak into existence life, and what you want to take place in your circumstance brought to the court – I speak healing to my body, finances to come to me, the justice of Yahweh to happen in this situation, etc.)

Amen, Thank You, Yahweh, for administrating court today. (1)

INTUITION GATE

I step into my intuition gate and allow the love of Yahweh to flood my intuition.

I connect my intuition to knowing the heart of Yahweh and His Kingdom Realms.

My intuition sees with the eyes of Yahweh's heart.

My intuition hears the intents of Yahweh's thoughts.

Ruach ha Kodesh, perfect my intuition, so I rightfully discern between good and evil.

Guide my intuition and lead me in Your pathways of understanding.

Yeshua seal my intuition with the light of love that illuminates from Your Being.

Hashilush ha Kodesh I submit my intuition to You. (1)

HEART INTERCESSION

I turn the intent of my heart to the Throne of Grace. I open my heart to You Yahweh.

Your love flows through my very being and penetrates the deep spaces of my intentions.

I surrender my desires and wants to Your heart that I may see like You see and speak what You speak.

As Your Son, I bring before You…(state the name of the person or speak the situation.)

I hold the person/situation in my heart that they/the situation may be immersed in Your love.

I wait to receive wisdom from You.

I wait to receive direction from You.

I will not act until I receive from You.

I am totally surrendered to Your will.

As I wait, holding the person/situation in my heart, I live in perfect Shalom.

BUILDING THE HOPE GATE

Yahweh, my hope is in You. My heart is glad, and You strengthen me to trust in You. (1)

I will hope continually, and I will praise You more and more and more. (2)

You are my hiding place and my shield. I hope in Your word. (3)

I am blessed because I trust and hope in You. (4)

Lord, You take pleasure in me because I fear You and hope in Your mercy. (5)

I know that hope does not disappoint because Your love is poured into my heart through Ruach Ha Kodesh (6)

I imprison myself in the Being of HOPE. You restore double unto me. (7)

You fill me with all-encompassing joy and peace, which causes me to abound in hope through Yeshua. (8)

As I speak hope, I AM HOPE. (9)

CONSCIENCE GATE

I step into my conscience gate. My conscience is alive, transformed by Your light and Your word, Yahweh. (1)

I align with Your heart bringing my conscience under Your powerful presence, Ruach ha Kodesh.

I embrace and engage the mysteries of Faith while keeping my conscience honorable, uncontaminated, and pure. (2)

Ruach ha Kodesh governs my conscience, so I live in and speak truth.

I completely belong to Hashilush ha Kodesh. (3)

Thank you, Yeshua, for offering Yourself as a perfect sacrifice.

I fully and thoroughly cleanse my conscience gate with Your sacred blood.

I am purified.

I am spotless.

I worship, love, and serve You with my devoted conscience. (4)

COMMUNION PRAYER

Yeshua, thank You for Your body that was sacrificed for me. Because I eat of it, it breaks the bonds of evil and brings me in the right position to rule and reign with You.

Offering Your body for me cleanses me from all sickness and sin, it changes my DNA to Your DNA, and I apply the sacrifice of Your body to split my soul and spirit.

The word is a two-edged sword piercing and splitting the soul and spirit. (1) I use that two-edged sword right now to split my soul and spirit.

Soul, you must bow to my spirit, you will NOT have dominion over it but my spirit will have dominion over you!

Yeshua, I take of this drink and take in Your blood that was shed for me. It heals any brokenness of soul, brings joy in my life, and turns me into a being of light.

I am totally immersed in You. You govern my soul, Ruach Hakodesh governs my body, and Yahweh governs my spirit.

I am righteous because of Your blood, and I'm cleansed of ALL sin. At this moment, I apply the power of Your body, blood, and resurrection to any situation I have today, and I am victorious in Yahweh! (2)

OX

I engage with the face of the Ox. (1)

The roaring of the Ox vibrates through the framework of my being penetrating every atom and cell.

It resonates with the calling to step into something greater.

I am called to be a Priest.

The burden bearer of ALL of Creation.

Through the ways of the Ox, I submit myself to the will of Yahweh. I am obedient to His call in my life.

I am patient and persevering to accomplish ALL that is written on my destiny scroll.

I operate alongside the Spirit of Might, displaying the strength of Yahweh in my purpose.

I am strong.

I am resolved.

I am the Ox hear me ROAR.

THE SPIRIT OF THE LORD

I turn the intent of my heart to befriend and call upon you Spirit of the Lord whose color is red.

I open my mind and heart to your instruction, which fashions me into the reflection of perfected Sonship.

I welcome and embrace your teaching, which enables me to see and experience the depth and breadth of Heaven's Realms.

I exercise dominion over the face of the Earth, bringing divine order.

I carry the glory of YHVH in the places and positions of authority He has given me.

I release justice and life from Heaven.

I accept Your mandate for my life YHVH and devote myself to Your flawless will.

Spirit of the Lord, I honor your position in my life.

Spirit of the Lord, I love you. (1)(2)

REASON GATE

Yahweh, I step before Your throne of grace at Your request. You asked me to come and reason together with You, so here I am in obedience and with sincerity.

You created me with the ability to think and reason, and as I plan my way, You establish my steps. (1)

I thank You for the measure of Faith You have given to me, letting my reasoning ability increase while allowing me to understand things I would never understand with reason alone. (2)

The give and take between my Emotion Gate and my Reason Gate creates balance within my soul and allows my body and spirit to engage in worship as my hands are raised in praise worshiping You in spirit and truth. (3)

I speak to my Reason Gateway, and I declare it will submit to my spirit.

As the love of Ruach ha Kodesh flows through the gateways of Worship and Faith and the Fear of Yahweh is firmly established in my spirit, my Reason Gateway is being cleansed of pride, self-righteousness, and conceit, (...add other vices that sit in this gate...).

With the blood of Yeshua, I wash away any residue from trading that sits in this gate. I declare I am free. Hallelujah. (4)

UNTETHERING FROM TIME

Yahweh, I present my body, soul, and spirit as a living sacrifice, and I admit and repent of... (do this prayer in the Mobile Court.)

When I unknowingly subjected myself to the passage of the sun through the 12 houses that have dictated my days where its voice has been speaking out to me, allowing it to cause my body to atrophy, where the radiation of the sun has become detrimental to me.

When I subjected myself to the moon and allowed it to strike me by night, causing me to be subjected to time, I unhook my DNA from being subject to the voice of the sun and moon.

When I've been subject to the 4 points of the compass and subjected myself to times and seasons, I unhook myself from it.

Where I have killed time, subjected myself to the north, south, east and west polls, seed-time and harvest, and the corruption of the Earth, I unhook myself from all of it.

Where I've been subject to the brooding of the Earth over me, the power of the seat of the solar system, subjected myself to the brooding over me of the stars, I unhook myself from it.

Where I've been subject to the brooding over me of the planet Mars, Venus, Uranus, Saturn, Mercury, Jupiter, Neptune, and all of their moons and/or suns, and any other planetary systems and any other dimensional engagements in the solar systems, I unhook myself from all of it.

I now ask that I be judged for this... (go through the other mobile court protocol.)

I now covenant to hook myself to the sound of Your voice that framed me from the beginning, to frame my body, and to frame the sun, moon, earth, and stars.

I hook myself to the sound of Your voice, that framed the north, south, east, and west polls, times and seasons, seed-time and harvest, the four points of the compass, the planetary systems in the cosmos and all-dimensional realms in the cosmos and I covenant to rule and reign over them as You have given me governance. (1)

ENGAGING THE ANGELIC REALM

I speak a Heavenly Portal where the Angelic Realm and Beings can enter from Heaven to Earth into my home.

Angels and Heavenly Beings you are welcome here. You are welcome in every room of my home. You can interact with my children and those who enter this house to bring the purposes of YHVH to pass.

Angels and Heavenly Beings, speak to me in the night season and during the day through cardiognosis, dreams, and visions when Yahweh wants to reveal His plans to me.

Being of Truth, Love, Joy, Holiness, and Rest you are welcome in my home.

Heavenly Realm, please use this place for your headquarters as you go back and forth on the earth.

Heavenly Beings, I welcome you here in this place.

STEPPING ON YOUR MOUNTAIN

In these last days, the mountain of The Lord's house is established on top of the mountains and is exalted above the hills. All of the nations flow to it. (1)

Yahweh, You have been my dwelling place throughout all of the generations. Before I was born, as a mountain, You brought forth the whole world. From everlasting to everlasting, You are my God. (2)

I am a Mountain that was born. The mountain of The Lord's house is established on the top of my mountain.

On my mountain sits a dais, a chair, where I rule and reign in Yahweh as a manifested Son. (3)

Above my mountain is the Angelic Canopy, where legions of Angels and Heavenly Beings are there to help me and guide me in my Sonship. I engage with the Angel assigned on my mountain to help me.

I engage with my mountain to encounter and enter the Kingdom Realms.

On my mountain I govern over the sphere of influence Yahweh has given me authority to govern over and bring the Will of Yahweh to pass in the earth and all of the cosmos.

WILL GATE

Yahweh, as I step into Your presence, I bow before Your throne. I submit my will to You because I am not born of the will of man but of You. (1) I train my will by meditating on Your word, which lights my path, allowing me to see my way clearly. (2)

Because my will is strong, I make positive choices that are revealed through my speech and actions bringing blessings to others.

I clean out my will gate as I take responsibility for not guarding it. I let go of stubbornness, short-sightedness, and self-defeating speech. I repent for allowing spirits that are not of You to have access through my will gate, and with the blood of Yeshua, I wipe this gateway clean and redeem it through the blood covenant of communion.

As I embrace the Kingdom lifestyle, I welcome Your love to flow through my First Love Gate into my being, leading me on the path towards mature Sonship. (3)

THE SPIRIT OF COUNSEL

I turn the intent of my heart to engage with the Spirit of Counsel, whose color is green.

Teach me about Hashilush ha Kodesh, Their role in me and around the world.

Teach me how to rule as a Son and how to access the councils of Yahweh.

Teach me how to consult with Yahweh and how to get to know Him as a friend.

Teach me the role of the royal advisors and the chancellors in the courts of Heaven.

Teach me about the cloud of witnesses, the men in white linen, and the role of those in the celestial realms.

Teach me how to facilitate who I am throughout ALL of Creation.

Spirit of counsel, I call you my friend.

Spirit of counsel, I love you. (1)

NOSE GATE

As I breathe in and out speaking the name of Yod Hey Vav Hey, I recognize the breath of His holiness in me. It is the breath of Yahweh in my nostrils. (1)

Yahweh has breathed the spirit of life into me.

With every breath I sing his praise and magnify his name.

I celebrate my creator, Who made the heavens. He breathed the Word, and the stars were born. (2)

With every breath that is in me, I raise a hallelujah, to Him who sits in glory and majesty.

My breath is like the wind, invisible, but with power I breathe the spirit of life into my home and my family creating all that is in my heart.

I open my heart to Yeshua, and the scent of roses engulfs me. It is the Rose of Sharon.

With joy, I inhale His wondrous aroma.

Today I thank Yahweh for breathing into my nostrils His breath... (3)

Because of You, I have LIFE.

Because of You, I have GRATITUDE.

Because of You, I AM ETERNAL.

EAGLE

I engage with the face of the Eagle. You are the Oracle, the utterance, the voice speaking the Word and carefully watching over it, brooding over it, and disciplining it until it prospers in its assignment. (1)

Eagle you expose the foundations of heavens government in which you sit, so I am learning to be an oracle in the earth; on earth as it is in Heaven.

You are the mouthpiece of the Kingdom, speaking the words of creation. Your words are like fire and a hammer breaking rocks into pieces, then bringing a different framework for something never seen before. (2) You are doing a new thing.

From the heavens, your eyes search the earth looking for me because I am fully committed to you, to take my seat of responsibility for creation. (3)

I am patiently waiting for you in this season as my old nature is stripped away, and a new being is emerging. (4) I look into the future and speak to creation, into the territory of my responsibility and terraform the earth.

As I gaze upon your face, I am transformed into you.

I AM AN EAGLE.

WISE.

CONFIDENT.

From glory to glory. (5) (6)

ENGAGING THE THRONE OF GRACE

I draw near to the Throne of Grace with confidence that Yahweh will have mercy and help me in my time of need. (1)

I am anxious about nothing because when I turn the intent of my heart to Yahweh, I make my requests known to Him. (2)

Your Throne Yahweh is forever and forever. The scepter of uprightness is the scepter of Your Kingdom. (3)

Yahweh, I sit in Your presence at the Throne of Grace. I totally immerse myself in Your Love. I speak to You as a Friend, step into Your Heart, and sit in the beauty of Your Holiness.

Here I am comforted and at rest. Here I am in perfect Shalom as the waves of Your Love flow over me again and again.

Here I am perfectly Yours.

MY IMAGINATION AS A GATE

I use the framework of my imagination as a gate to step through and see Yeshua, my Shephard.

He shows me a soft green pasture where I relax with Him and rest.

I feel the warm gentle breeze blowing over me, and I hear the sweet melody of the water.

I fear nothing.

I yield to You.

I am anointed with oil.

My cup overflows.

Your goodness and mercy are Everlasting.

I AM SHALOM (1)(2)

THE SPIRIT OF KNOWLEDGE

Spirit of Knowledge whose color is indigo, I turn the intent of my heart to engage with you friend to friend.

By your instruction, you show me how to access the knowledge of Yahweh.

You enable me to gain access to the knowledge of the Kingdom Realms.

You instruct me how to retain the knowledge I've learned so I may use it for the will and glory of Yahweh.

You also teach me how to meditate and receive divine insight into the secrets and mysteries of Yahweh's heart

Spirit of Knowledge I seek you to help me learn and grow in my spiritual maturity as a Son.

You are the one I consult for information.

You are the one that helps me grow.

You are the one I seek to know. (1)

CHOICE GATE

I turn the intent of my heart to You Yahweh, as I choose to serve You with my heart, soul, and mind. I choose abundant life. I choose to live as I declare Your sovereignty over me and my house. (1)

Because my choices train my soul, my soul responds to Your Kingdom, and so I choose to forgive freely, allowing me to be in right standing before You. (2)

I choose to be joyful. I choose to react positively to every circumstance that confronts me. I choose to take responsibility for my words and actions. I choose to be a victor. I choose to accomplish everything I set out to do with excellence and integrity.

Yahweh, I choose to create a platform in my life that You will be pleased with and that You will sit on. I choose to sit in my seat of authority and bring what is in Heaven onto the earth. (3)

I choose to give Ruach ha Kodesh influence over all my choices. (4)

MAN

I engage with who Yahweh made me to be...Man.

I am made to connect and relate to my emotions and feelings.

It gives me the ability to love, relate to other beings, and be vulnerable.

Because I am a man, I can share the deepest desires of my heart and listen to others share their deepest desires with me.

I long for intimacy with others.

A relational connection that grows through eternity.

I relate by touch, smell, feeling, and seeing.

My heart yearns for the friendship of Yahweh.

My heart yearns for the friendship of Yeshua.

My heart yearns for the friendship of Ruach ha Kodesh.

My heart yearns for intimacy with the Hashilush ha Kodesh. (1)

OPENING MY LOVE GATE

I step into the love gate, my most secret place, the place where I engage with my Father, Yahweh.

This is the GARDEN OF MY HEART.

The place where I meet Yeshua.

The place where I meet Ruach ha Kodesh.

At the entrance of my heart, I reserve this place for Them that WE may grow in relationship, friendship, and intimacy.

At the entrance are guardian angels that protect this gate because out of it flows the power source that fuels every other gate.

Love is the power source—love from the heart of Yahweh.

Love that is ETERNAL.

Love that never fails.

Love the pulses through every aspect of my being.

Love that restores.

Love that makes ALL THINGS NEW.

The love of Hashilush ha Kodesh.

I LOVE YOU... (1)

ENGAGING THE GATE OF REVELATION

Yahweh, it is Your glory to conceal revelation, and my duty as a King to search it out. (1)

You reveal the secrets embedded in the high places and the mysteries hidden in the depths below.

I thirst for the revealing of more of You.

I choose the letters formed from Your voice to fish in the sea of mysteries and darkness.

Your light reveals the truth of who You are and the expanse of your righteousness.

Engaging with the treasures of Your revelation is where I sit.

I open my Being to receive more, and more, and more, and more... (2)

I AM A THREE-PART BEING

I AM A THREE-PART BEING...

My spirit is the first being, implanted in the womb of my mother by Ruach ha Kodesh.

My spirit is connected to the spirit of Yahweh. It knows the revelation of my destiny, who I am in Yahweh, and the blueprint of my creation.

My body is the second being, fashioned from the gold dust of the ground. Inside my body which is the temple of Yahweh lives Ruach ha Kodesh.

I engage in the presence of righteousness, and the power of Ruach ha Kodesh heals my body.

I am formed by the hands of Yahweh, beautifully sculpted from the creation of His heart and mind.

My soul is the third being, created when Yahweh entered into me and exhaled the breath of life.

In my soul resides Yeshua, Who works sanctification in me.

Right now, I choose to surrender my three-part being to its original design and purpose.

I do not choose death but choose life; to live for eternity. (1)

EMOTION GATE

I step into the gate of emotion and feel Your heartbeat, Yahweh, echoing in the depths of my being.

You made me in Your image and rejoiced in Your handiwork. (1)

I place my emotions under the canopy of Ruach ha Kodesh, Who governs my heart and soul.

I cleanse my emotions gate with the blood of Yeshua.

I am corrected and directed in the framing of my emotions.

They are the holy expression of light and truth.

I release the sound of a new song from my lips, uttering your praises.

It excites the atmosphere around me with joy, so many trust in Yahweh. (2) (3)

ACTIVATING MY GODHOOD

MY DNA is the wholeness of YHVH. EVERY part of my BODY AND ITS CELLULAR MEMORY IS IN PERFECT HEALTH, transforming MY BODY into the flawless, SINLESS AGE of... (put your optimal age here.)

MY DNA is the vibration, frequency, sound, fragrance, light, and Alef-Beis of Yahweh, where I can manipulate and speak MATTER into existence and my body can create a black hole which allows me to travel in and out of time, AT WILL to different realms, terrestrially, celestially, dimensionally and other ways YHVH sees fit.

MY SOUL IS PERFECTED, formed in the IMAGE OF YHSVH, without spot or blemish, pure and holy, embodying the righteousness, joy, and peace of Ruach Hakodesh, speaking Love and Truth.

MY SPIRT IS THE SPIRIT OF YHVH, operating as the Lead vessel of my three-part being, understanding and speaking the secrets and mysteries of YHVH, knowing ALL THINGS, bringing His WILL operating through my SOUL, AND BODY ON Earth and ALL OF CREATION.

THE SPIRIT OF WISDOM

Spirit of Wisdom whose color is orange, I turn the intent of my heart to engage with you friend to friend.

Equip me for the position as a Son of YHVH.

In you is prosperity, delight, and true judgement.

In you is joy, contentment, and the total fulfillment of Yahweh.

Teach me how to exercise the authority, dominion, and power given to me by Yahweh.

Teach me the wisdom of Yahweh in all things.

I surrender the wisdom of my soul and seek the wisdom of you and your handmaidens.

Spirit of Wisdom I seek you in the day.

Spirit of Wisdom I seek you in the night.

Spirit of Wisdom, you are my friend.

Spirit of Wisdom, I love you. (1)

I AM FREQUENCY

I am a vibration, frequency, and sound created by Yahweh.

The original design of my cells was created to move in circular patterns perfectly formed from the intent and purpose of Yahweh to have dominion over all of creation.

The vibration of my cells gives the sweet fragrance of the aroma of Heaven.

My cells have a tune that is distinct, unique, and one of a kind.

Yahweh calls to me with the frequency of His Being.

I vibrate back the sound of my being.

Together we create one tune in absolute harmony.

My cells vibrate at a megahertz that radiates immaculate health, joy, and peace.

My frequency creates white light piercing the darkness of mysteries yet to be revealed. (1)

MIND GATE

I step into my mind gate to be transformed and renewed by the washing of the blood of Yeshua.

I place a guard at my mind to examine everything I see.

I am able to discern Your good and perfect will, Yahweh. (1)

I keep my mind anchored in You Lord, so Shalom blankets my conscious, subconscious, and unconscious.

I daily meditate on Your word day and night, which envelops my mind with the wonder of You. (2)

Your voice fashions my body so I function according to Your will.

I yield my neurological pathways redesigning my thinking to entangle with Your light and love.

My thoughts flame as a lamp shining to enfold Your glory for my soul to encounter. (3) (4)

REIGNING IN REST

Yahweh, I turn the intent of my heart to You and thank You for Your promise of the rest You have provided. I enter Your rest, which is freely offered, and as I sit on the seat of my mountain, reigning as a King, I am at rest. (1)

I do not need rest from work or physical exhaustion because You give me a profound sense of peace through Your heart of compassion, mercy, grace, and love. You teach me to extend these qualities as I govern those You give me authority over.

I position myself in Your heart, and the intimacy WE experience moves me into rest. Your presence in me creates the capacity to be still and quiet. In this stillness, I see Your face and am empowered to engage my destiny with a clear vision.

At rest, I govern over times and seasons, over the frequency that I live in and change the reality of who I am.

I surrender myself to Your perfect will and frame my future in the reality of Your creation because I am at rest in You. (2)

WISDOM OF THE REALMS

I engage with Wisdom of the realms brought forth by the mouth of Yahweh in the beginning of His ways. (1)

Before His works of old you were fashioned in Him.

For you are better than rubies.

You were set up from everlasting, from the beginning before all of creation and the earth was made.

You dwell with prudence, and find knowledge of witty inventions.

You were there when Yahweh established the heavens and the earth with the sound of His voice.

You are a delight, daily before Yahweh.

I am your delight as a Son of Yahweh.

So, I turn my heart to listen to your instruction.

I watch daily at your gates and wait patiently at your doors.

I look for you, so I look for life.

I yearn to keep your ways.

Wisdom of the Realms I love you...

HAND GATE

I lift my hands in praise to Adonai (1), Who affirms the work of my hands. (2)

Because of Your great Love for me, I am sure of Your care for me as a loving Father.

You watched me during my fetal development and then engraved my name on Your palm. (3)

Adonai, Your right hand holds me up, thus preventing me from falling, so I bless You and lift my hands in worship. (4)

As I step into the heart of You, You show me how to purify my heart.

It reflects Yours, so I experience success in what I do.

When I endeavor to work, my hands never fumble, and I complete every assignment with excellence.

Hands you have been designed by Adonai in an amazing way. You have the ability to clap in applause, raise in worship, and create using things in nature. With clay, you make vessels, with seeds you plant and harvest, with wood you build and sculpt, and then you fold in thanks and prayer to Adonai.

Hands, you have been fearfully and wonderfully made and I bow in praise and thanks to Adonai. (5) (6)

THE SPIRIT OF MIGHT

I turn the intent of my heart to engage with the Spirit of Might whose color is blue. I step into the Court of War and Strategy and come to access the strategies that you teach me.

You reveal my position, and with this knowledge and strength, I begin to work out my destiny scroll as I present my authorized mandate. (1)

You teach me how to sit on my mountain, and from there, I exercise my authority from the supernatural realm and bring the Kingdom of Yahweh into the natural realm.

I honor you as you instruct me about the rulership of my seat as it relates to the seat of the Mountain of Yahweh that is above me. (2)

As you unfold for me the POWER and DOMINION of YHVH and how He exercises His authority, I create a platform on the earth that mirrors what is in Heaven so that the power and authority of Yahweh can be manifest through me on the earth. (3)

I thank you, Spirit of Might that you are on my side, and as the mysteries are revealed, you reveal me for my position, providing me with a way to war in both the natural and celestial arenas. (4)

HEAVENLY TRADING

Yahweh, I step through the veil and stand in awe before Your throne in total surrender because of a trade You agreed to, in order to save me.

Yeshua, with heartfelt gratitude, I bow at Your feet in thankfulness for the trade You made, giving Your life in exchange for mine.

This is indeed, the ultimate trade.

Yeshua, the sacrifice of Your body gives me the promise of healing for my body. (1) As I take communion daily, I claim this promise - I declare that I will not die but live and declare Your glory. (2)

I step onto the Sea of Glass, and as the elders cast their crowns before Yahweh, I trade my communion for a deeper, more intimate relationship with You. (3)

I breathe in every breath you exhale, for Your breath gives me life. (4)

Today I trade my time, my talents and my finances into Your Kingdom and treasure is stored for me as Your blessings pour down. (5)

At this moment, I turn my heart in worship to You.

Seeking Your heart. I give myself to You, and in return, I experience intense intimacy encompassing love, joy, peace, patience, kindness, goodness, faithfulness, and self-control. (6)

YHSVH You are all that I need.
I step into Your name with humility.
I desire face-to-face encounters, and I am filled. (7)
Hinehni - Lord here I am. (8)

FEAR OF YHVH GATE

I step into the Fear of YHVH gate.

I set my heart and eyes to reflect upon You.

I tremble in the Fear of You because of Who You Are...

I AM IN AWE AND WONDER....

I AM IN AWE AND AMAZEMENT...

I AM IN AWE AND FEAR...

With great honor, humiliation, and love, I recognize Your Perfection.

Your love does not change.

Your ways do not change.

You are the same today, yesterday and tomorrow. (1)

With all that is in me, I claim, The Fear of You is the beginning of wisdom and the knowledge of You is everything I will ever need. (2) (3)

REFERENCES

SPEAKING LIFE – (1) Psalms 8:5-6; (2) Proverbs 18:21; (3) Ephesians 4:29; (4) Job 22:28; (5) Mark 4:26; (6) Proverbs 13:2-3; (7) Deuteronomy 28:1-13.

MOUTH GATE – (1) Proverbs 10:19, 21: (2) Ephesians 4:29; (3) Proverbs 21:23; (4) Colossians 4:6; (5) This prayer is based on the book by Ian Clayton, *Gateways of The Threefold Nature of Man.*

THE AGE OF MELCHIZEDEK – (1) This prayer is based on the Ian Clayton teaching entitled, *The Ages,* found at **www.sonofthunder.org**

THE SPIRIT OF THE FEAR OF THE LORD – (1) Proverbs 14:27; (2) 2 Corinthians 5:11, Proverbs 22:4; (3) Proverbs 14:26, Proverbs 19:23; (4) Isaiah 33:6.

ENGAGING THE BEING OF FAITH – (1) Matthew 17:20; (2) Numbers 23:19; (3) Philippians 3:9; (4) Matthew 16:19; (5) Joshua 1:8.

EYE GATE – (1) Matthew 6:22; (2) Job 31:1; (3) Psalms 101:3. (4) This prayer is based on the book by Ian Clayton, *Gateways of The Threefold Nature of Man.*

EXPANDING YOUR SPIRIT MAN – (1) John 7:38; (2) This prayer is based on the Ian Clayton teaching entitled, *Family Life,* found at **www.sonofthunder.org**

WORSHIP GATE – (1) This prayer is based on the book by Ian Clayton, *Gateways of The Threefold Nature of Man.*

REVERANCE GATE – (1) Malachi 2:5; (2) Genesis 17:3; (3) Romans 14:8; (4) Isaiah 26:4; (5) This prayer is based on the book by Ian Clayton, *Gateways of The Threefold Nature of Man.*

LION – (1) This prayer is based on the book by Ian Clayton, *Realms of the Kingdom, Vol. 2, Chapter 6, The Four Faces of God.*

ANI (I AM) – (1) Ephesians 5:27 (2) 1 Corinthians 6:19.

EAR GATE – (1) Job 36:10; (2) Proverbs 2:2; (3) Isaiah 30:21; (4) Mark 4:23-24 (5) This prayer is based on the book by Ian Clayton, *Gateways of The Threefold Nature of Man.*

MOBILE COURT ENGAGEMENT – (1) This prayer is based on the Ian Clayton teaching entitled, *The Mobile Court,* found at **www.sonofthunder.org**.

INTUITION GATE - (1) This prayer is based on the book by Ian Clayton, *Gateways of The Threefold Nature of Man.*

BUILDING THE HOPE GATE – (1) Psalms 16:9 and 31:24; (2) Psalms 71:5 and 14. (3) Psalms 119:114; (4) Jeremiah 17:7; (5) Psalms 147:11. (6) Romans 5:5; (7) Zechariah 9:12; (8) Romans 15:13.; (9) This prayer is based on the book by Ian Clayton, *Gateways of The Threefold Nature of Man.*

CONSCIENCE GATE – (1) Psalms 19:8; (2) 1 Timothy 3:9; (3) Romans 9:1; (4) This prayer is based on the book by Ian Clayton, *Gateways of The Threefold Nature of Man.*

COMMUNION PRAYER – (1) Hebrews 4:12 (2) This prayer is based on the Ian Clayton teaching entitled, *Communion,* found at **www.sonofthunder.org.**

OX – (1) This prayer is based on the book by Ian Clayton, *Realms of the Kingdom, Vol. 2, Chapter 6, The Four Faces of God.*

SPIRIT OF THE LORD – (1) This prayer is based on the Mike Parson teaching about the 7 Spirits of YHVH at **www.eg.freedomarc.org.** (2) This prayer is based on the book by Ian Clayton, *Realms of the King-*

dom, Vol. 1.

REASON GATE – (1) Isaiah 1:18; Proverbs 16:9; (2) Romans 12:3; (3) John 4:23-24; (4) This prayer is based on the book by Ian Clayton, *Gateways of The Threefold Nature of Man.*

UNTERTHERING FROM TIME – (1) This prayer is written from the Ian Clayton teaching entitled, *Unhooked from Time,* found at **www.sonofthunder.org**

STEPPING ON YOUR MOUNTAIN – (1) Isaiah 2:2; (2) Psalms 90:1-2; (3) Romans 8:19.

WILL GATE – (1) John 1:13; (2) Joshua 1:8; (3) This prayer is based on the book by Ian Clayton, *Gateways of The Threefold Nature of Man.*

THE SPIRIT OF COUNSEL – (1) This prayer is based on the Mike Parson teaching about the 7 Spirits of YHVH at **www.eg.freedomarc.org**.

NOSE GATE – (1) Job 27:3; (2) Psalms 33:6; (3) This prayer is based on the book by Ian Clayton, *Gateways of The Threefold Nature of Man.*

EAGLE – (1) Isaiah 55:11; (2) Jeremiah 23: 29; (3) 2 Chronicles 16:9; (4) Isaiah 40:31; (5) 2 Corinthians 3:18; (6) This prayer is based on the book by Ian

Clayton, *Realms of the Kingdom, Vol. 2, Chapter 6, The Four Faces of God,* and the book, *The Order of Melchizedek.*

ENGAGING THE THRONE OF GRACE – (1) Hebrews 4:16; (2) Philippians 4:6; (3) Hebrews 1:8.

MY IMAGINATION AS A GATE – (1) Psalms 23; (2) This prayer is based on the book by Ian Clayton, *Gateways of The Threefold Nature of Man.*

THE SPIRIT OF KNOWLEDGE – (1) This prayer is based on the Mike Parson teaching about the 7 Spirits of YHVH at **www.eg.freedomarc.org**.

CHOICE GATE – (1) Deuteronomy 30:19; (2) Psalms 118:17; (3) Matthew 6:10; (4) This prayer is based on the book by Ian Clayton, *Gateways of The Threefold Nature of Man.*

MAN – (1) This prayer is based on the book by Ian Clayton, *Realms of the Kingdom, Vol. 1.*

OPENING MY LOVE GATE – (1) This prayer is based on the book by Ian Clayton, *Gateways of The Threefold Nature of Man.*

ENGAGING THE GATE OF REVELATION – (1) Proverbs 25:2; (2) This prayer is based on the book by Ian

Clayton, *Gateways of The Threefold Nature of Man.*

I AM A THREE-PART BEING – (1) This prayer is based on the book by Ian Clayton, *Gateways of The Threefold Nature of Man.*

EMOTION GATE – (1) Psalms 104:31; (2) Psalms 40:3; (3) This prayer is based on the book by Ian Clayton, *Gateways of The Threefold Nature of Man.*

THE SPIRIT OF WISDOM – (1) This prayer is based on the Mike Parson teaching about the 7 Spirits of YHVH at **www.eg.freedomarc.org**.

I AM FREQUENCY – (1) This prayer is based on the Ian Clayton teaching, *The Frequency of Our Thoughts*, found at **www.sonofthunder.org.**

MIND GATE – (1) Romans 12:2; (2) Joshua 1:8; (3) 2 Peter 1:19; (4) This prayer is based on the book by Ian Clayton, *Gateways of The Threefold Nature of Man.*

REIGNING IN REST – (1) Hebrews 4: 1-8; (2) This prayer is based on the Ian Clayton teaching entitled, *The Way of Rest,* found at **www.sonofthunder.org.**

WISDOM OF THE REALMS – (1) Proverbs 8.

HAND GATE – (1) Psalms 134:2; (2) Psalms 90:17; (3) Isaiah 49:16; (4) Psalms 63:4, 8; (5) Psalms 139:14; (6) This prayer is based on the book by Ian Clayton, *Gateways of The Threefold Nature of Man.*

SPIRIT OF MIGHT – (1) Ephesians 3:16; (2) Isaiah 2:2; (3) Job 12:13-14; (4) This prayer is based on the Mike Parson teaching about the 7 Spirits of YHVH at **www.eg.freedomarc.org**.

HEAVENLY TRADING – (1) Isaiah 53:5; (2) Psalms 118:17; 1 Corinthians 11:23-30; (3) Revelation 4:10-11; (4) Job 33:4; (5) Malachi 3:10-12; (6) Jeremiah 29: 13; Galatians 5:22-23; (7) Philippians 2:10. (8) This prayer is based on the book by Ian Clayton, *Realms of The Kingdom Vol 2.*

FEAR OF YHVH GATE – (1) Hebrews 13:8; (2) Proverbs 9:10; (3) This prayer is based on the book by Ian Clayton, *Gateways of The Threefold Nature of Man.*

ABOUT THE AUTHORS

Ruth C. Forde is a native of Zimbabwe with roots in South Africa. She holds a teaching diploma in early childhood education from the Bulawayo Teachers College in Zimbabwe, a Bachelor of Science degree in Education from Walla Walla University in Washington State and has studied for a Master's degree in Curriculum Development from La Sierra University in California.

Ruth Forde is an educator and has taught in the elementary school system of the United States for twenty-five plus years. She has extensive experience in teaching the under-privileged and disadvantaged children. However, she considers her most rewarding achievement in the area of spiritual growth.

She has learned the "deep things of God" and her spiritual journey has been so rewarding it has become her passion. Ruth believes we should be living supernatural lives here and now. Ruth is married to Nathan Forde a native of Chicago Illinois, and has two adult children.

Nina L. Hayden is a graduate of Stetson University College of Law where she received her Doctorate Degree, J.D. in 2003 and Masters of Law, LL.M Degree in International Law in 2012. She worked at the Office of the Public Defender, Sixth Judicial Circuit. After working at the Office of the Public Defender she worked as a Solo Practitioner and for Stetson University College of Law as a Professor of Practice and Director of Bar Preparation and Academic Success. She has also taught as an Adjunct Professor at the University of Tampa.

Nina's community work includes many hours of work with public school students through various mentoring programs. She has sat on many boards throughout the community including the Police Athletic League in Lealman. Nina ran for office and was elected to the Pinellas County School Board in 2008 where she served for 2 years. After serving on the School Board she ran for the FL State Senate in 2010 and U.S. House District 10 seat in 2012.

Nina moved to Pinellas County Florida in 1998. She is the youngest of four siblings and has a twin sister who lives in Italy with her husband. However, most of all, she enjoys encouraging others to develop a deeper walk with Yahweh.

Mary J. Ottmann-Bass is a native of Toronto, Canada where she attended Ryerson Polytechnical Institute for their Theater program. She attained the position of assistant coach for stage combat choreography and dance classes. She also taught stage production make-up and design. In 1979 Mary moved to the United States to pursue her acting career with the Hilberry Theater Company at Wayne State University in Detroit Michigan, where she performed in numerous Shakespeare and contemporary productions.

Soon thereafter, Mary moved to New York to continue her theater career performing in children's productions, doing voice over work and acting in a children's television show filmed in Canada. During her time in New York opportunities came about which lead Mary into the business world where she functioned in management.

Mary has a passion for encouraging others to pursue their growth in Yahweh to fulfill who they are created to be. While living in FL she immersed herself in ministry for many years. She is married to William A. Bass a native of Tulsa, Oklahoma. They have two children and four dogs.

Ruth C. Forde, Nina L. Hayden, and Mary J. Ottmann-Bass are Co-founders of Godzwow, Inc., Godzwow Publications Inc, and Shaar Lamed, Inc. They are passionate about growing the body of Yeshua into a deeper walk with the heart of Yahweh.

Published by Godzwow Publications, Inc.

www.godzwowpublications.com

Manufactured by Amazon.ca
Bolton, ON